Basic Instructions for All Projects

Use your choice of closures and chains on any bracelet or necklace.

Hook and Eye Closure with Double Loop Chain.

Toggle and Eye Closure with S - Loop Chain.

Closures

Hooks

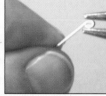 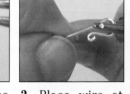 

1. Bend down one end and press to form a half loop. (Each hook uses about 1¹/2" of wire.)

2. Place wire at the middle of pliers shank. Bend wire over shank.

3. Turn a loop in the other end of the wire to attach the hook.

Eyes

1. Begin about ¹/8" from one end to bend down one end to form a ¹/3" loop.
2. Turn a small loop. Wrap the end of the wire around both wires. Cut away any excess wire. (Each loop uses about 3" of wire.)

Toggles

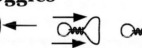

1. Make an eye as instructed above. Press on the top of the larger loop to flatten it.
2. Pinch the larger loop with flat nose pliers to flatten the loop to form a tall thin loop. Insert the toggle into an eye. (Each uses about 3" of wire.)

Chain Styles

S - Hook

Make an S-hook according to the instructions on page. Twist one loop flat. (Each loop uses about 1" of wire.)

Pretzel

Fold wire ends across the center. Twist one loop flat. (Each loop uses about 1" of wire.)

Double Loop

Turn a loop in the end of the wire. Turn another loop over the first one. Make another loop about ¹/4" away. Bend the wire end to the center of the double loops. Twist the long loop flat. (Each loop uses about 2" of wire.)

Bead

Loop Bead Units

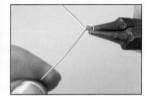

1. Use round nose pliers to turn a loop in one end. To begin loop, bend down ³/8" of wire.
2. Grasp wire end with pliers and roll it around to form a circle. Thread bead and turn a loop in the other end. (Each loop bead unit uses 1 to 2" of wire.)

Wrap Bead Units

Wrap bead units are stronger than loop bead units.

1. Thread a bead onto the wire. Use round nose pliers to bend down ³/8" of wire.

2. Roll the wire into a loop and wrap the short end around the long end 4-5 times.

3. Pull bead up into place and turn another loop in the wire about ¹/4" from the bead.

4. Wrap the end of the wire around the wire beside the bead 4 or 5 times. Trim wire.

(Each wrap bead unit uses about 2" of wire.)

S - Hooks

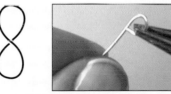 

1. Use round nose pliers to turn a loop in one end of the wire.
2. Turn another loop in the opposite direction at the other end of the wire. (Each loop uses about 1" of wire.)

Coils or Jump Rings

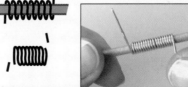 

1. Hold a dowel, skewer, crochet hook or knitting needle in one hand. Press your thumb against the wire and dowel. Use the other hand to wrap wire tightly 4 times.

2. Remove coil from the dowel and cut off the ends of the wire. If desired, make a longer coil by using more wire and cut the coil as necessary to make the length desired. **Tip** - Cut coils apart to make jump rings.

continued on page 5

Simply Loops

Have you every played with a soda straw or a blade of grass - twirling it into little circles and loops around your fingers? You have?!? Great!

You already know how to make the looped wire shapes that go into each project shown below - and you are well on your way to completing every project in this book! Let's get started!

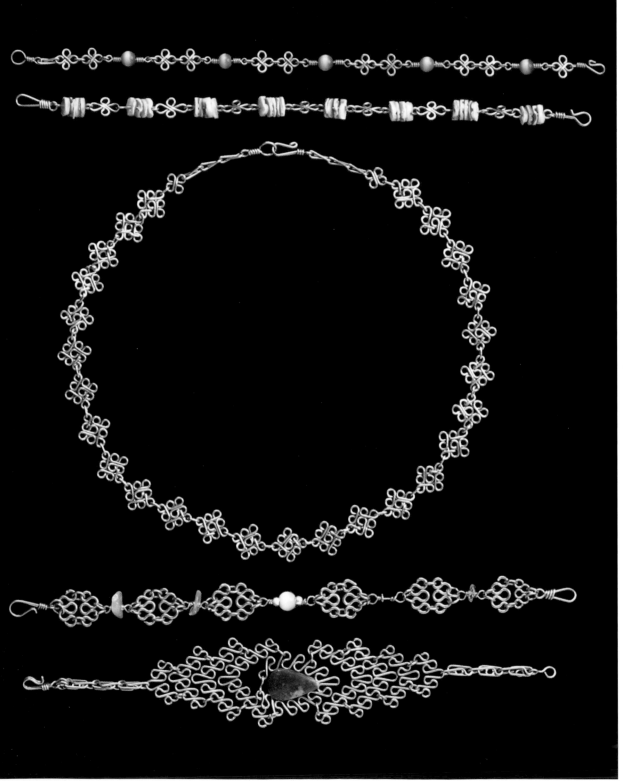

Cloverleaf & Cat's Eye Beads Bracelet

MATERIALS:
20 gauge Silver wire • 5 Olive Green 5mm cat's eye beads • 16 jump rings
INSTRUCTIONS: Thread beads on wire. Make 5 wrap bead units (see page 3). Turn a loop and wrap around the wire 4 times. Slide a bead to the center of shape. Wrap around the wire. Cut off the end. (Each bead unit uses about 2" of wire).

Make 10 cloverleafs. Attach pieces with jump rings. (Each cloverleaf. uses about 2" of wire).

Make 5 bead units.

Make 11 cloverleaves.

Cloverleaf & Shell Beads Bracelet -

MATERIALS:
20 gauge Silver wire • 32 puka shell beads • jump rings
INSTRUCTIONS: Make 8 bead units using 4 shell beads for each one (see page 3). Turn a loop in one end of the wire. Slide 4 beads to the center of the shape. Turn a loop at the end then cut off excess wire. (Each bead unit uses 2" of wire).

Make 7 cloverleafs with longer side petals. Attach pieces. (Each cloverleaf uses about 2" of wire).

Make 8 bead units.

Make 7 cloverleafs.

9-Circle Leaves Necklace -

MATERIALS: 20 gauge Silver wire • 27 jump rings
INSTRUCTIONS: Turn a loop at one end of the wire - this is the center. Make another loop beside the first one. Make a loop above and between the other 2 circles. Make a loop in line with the last 2 loops. Continue making loops in the wire around the center to form a tilted square. Trim off any excess wire. (Each 9-circle leaf uses about 4" of wire.).

Make 26 of the 9- circle leaves. Make 2 clover leafs.
Attach pieces with jump rings.

 Turn a loop in the end of the wire to make the center circle of the leaf.

Turn a loop next to the first one. This is the left corner of the leaf.

Turn a loop above the first 2 circles.

Turn another loop above the first one for the top circle.

Continue turning loops around each side. End below and between the first 2 circles.

Wiggles & Stones Bracelet -

MATERIALS: 20 gauge Silver wire • Pink 6mm pearl bead • 2 Silver 2mm beads • 4 Pink 6mm crystal beads • 36 jump rings
INSTRUCTIONS: Make a wrap bead unit (see page 3) using a 6mm bead.

Make 4 wrapped bead units using a crystal bead for each one. (Each bead unit uses about 2" of wire).

Make 12 wiggles as shown. (Each wiggle uses about 4" of wire).

Join bead units to wiggles with 2 jump rings.

Attach 2 wiggles together with a jump ring in the first loop on each side of wiggles.

Join bead units to wiggles with 2 jump rings.

Make 1 bead unit with the Silver beads and the pearl. Wrap the wire twice at either side.

Make 4 bead units with the crystals. Wrap the wire 4 times on either side.

Turn 5 loops to make each wiggle. Make 12 wiggles.
Join pairs of wiggles with jump rings.

Flames & Stone Bracelet -

MATERIALS: 20 gauge Silver wire • 1 Blue 16 x 10mm stone • 16 jump rings
INSTRUCTIONS: Make two 9-loop wiggles. Turn a loop and turn another loop below and to the right of the first one. Make 2 more back-and-forth loops. Bend the wire to make the center loop. Repeat to turn 4 loops in a mirror image of the first 4 loops. Cut off excess wire. (Each 9-loop wiggle requires about 5" of wire).

Make two 13-loop wiggles.. Turn a loop and turn another loop below and to the right of the first one. Make 4 more back-and-forth loops. Bend the wire to make the center loop. Repeat to turn 4 loops in a mirror image of the first 4 loops. Cut off excess wire. (Each 13-loop wiggle uses about 7" of wire).

Make two 17-loop wiggles. Turn 8 loops above and below the center loop. (Each 17-loop wiggle requires about 9" of wire).

Make two 21-loop wiggles. Turn 10 loops above and below the center loop. (Each 21-loop wiggle uses about 12" of wire).

Make loops that wrap around the center stone. (Uses about 15" of wire).
Attach pieces with jump rings.

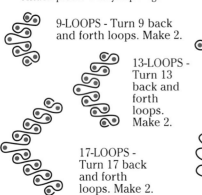

9-LOOPS - Turn 9 back and forth loops. Make 2.

13-LOOPS - Turn 13 back and forth loops. Make 2.

17-LOOPS - Turn 17 back and forth loops. Make 2.

21-LOOPS - Turn 21 back and forth loops. Make 2.

CENTER - Turn 27 back and forth loops to make a flame strip 2" long. Bend the strip around the stone. Secure the end loops with an S hook. Glue wire to stone.

Basic Shapes
continued from page 3

Use round nosed pliers to make all shapes.

Jump Ring

1. Wrap wire around a dowel or crochet needle to make a tight coil. Use wire cutters to cut rings apart. (See page 3)

2. Use 1 or two jump rings to attach elements together. Alternate 1 jump ring with 2 jump rings to make an attractive chain.

Cloverleaf

1. Turn a loop in the end of the wire to make the first petal of a cloverleaf.

2. Turn a loop above and to the right of the first petal. This forms the top petal.

3. Turn a loop at the right side for the third petal.

4. Turn a loop at the bottom for the last petal.
(Each cloverleaf requires about 2" of wire.)

Spiral

1. Use the tips of the round nose pliers to turn a small loop in the end of the wire.

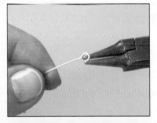

2. Wrap the tips of the flat nose pliers with tape to keep from scratching wire. Grasp the loop with flat nose pliers. Hold the wire flat with one hand and turn the pliers to wrap the wire around the center loop.

3. Cover an anvil with a paper towel. Place a spiral on the anvil and tap it with a hammer to flatten it. Do not hammer top loops.
(Each spiral requires about 3" of wire.)

Bead Dangles

Delicate beads that hang from a variety of wire shapes make a colorful addition to your wardrobe.

Your friends who would love a personalized contribution to their accessories cache, too!

Turquoise Beads Necklace -

MATERIALS: 20 gauge Silver wire • 15 Turquoise 6mm beads • 15 Silver 3mm beads • jump rings

INSTRUCTIONS: Make 7 bead units (see page 3). Slide a bead to the center of the wire. Wrap one end of the wire around the wire above the bead. Cut off the end. Slide a silver bead onto the other end of wire. Turn a loop in the end of the wire. (Each bead unit uses about 2" of wire).

Make chain with jump rings. Attach bead units.

Thread a bead to the center of the wire.

Wrap one wire around the other one 3 times.

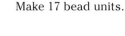

Add a 3mm bead, loop the end of the wire.

Cloverleaf and Green Pearls Necklace -

MATERIALS: 20 gauge Silver wire • 17 Light Green 5mm pearls • jump rings

INSTRUCTIONS: Make 17 bead units (see page 3). Turn a loop in one end of the wire. Slide a bead to the center of the wire. Turn a loop in the other end of the wire. (Each bead unit uses about 2" of wire).

Make 19 cloverleafs. Attach a bead unit to 17 cloverleaf. Use the other 2 cloverleafsat the end of the outer beads. (Each cloverleaf uses about 2" of wire)

Make 17 bead units.

Make 19 cloverleafs. Attach each bead unit to a cloverleaf.

Cloverleaf and Lavender Crystals Necklace -

MATERIALS: 20 gauge Silver wire • 17 Lavender 5mm x 3mm crystal beads • 17 Silver 3mm beads • jump rings

INSTRUCTIONS: Make 17 bead units (see page 3). Turn a loop in one end of the wire. Slide a crystal and Silver bead onto the wire. Turn a loop in the other end of the wire. (Each bead unit uses about 2" of wire)

Make 19 cloverleaves. (Each cloverleaf uses about 2" of wire)

Attach a bead unit to 13 cloverleafs. Use the other 3 cloverleafs on each side of necklace.

Attach cloverleafs together with jump rings..

Make 17 bead units.
Make 19 cloverleafs.
Attach each bead unit to a cloverleaf.

Cloverleaf and Pearly Stones Necklace -

MATERIALS: 20 gauge Silver wire • 28 Mother of Pearl 7mm x 3mm stones • 21 Silver 3mm beads • 2 Mother of Pearl 6mm beads • E6000 glue • jump rings

INSTRUCTIONS: Make 17 bead units (see page 3). Turn a loop in one end of the wire. Slide 2 stones and and a Silver bead up the wire. Turn a loop in the other end of the wire. (Each bead unit uses about 2" of wire).

Make 2 wrapped bead units. Turn a loop in one end of the wire and wrap the wire end under the loop. Slide 1 Silver, 1 stone and 1 Silver bead up the wire. Turn a loop and wrap the other end of the wire.

Make 2 wrapped bead units. Turn a loop in one end of the wire and wrap the wire end under the loop. Slide 1 Silver, a 6mm bead and 1 Silver bead up the wire. Turn a loop and wrap the other end of the wire.

Make 15 cloverleafs. Attach a double stone unit to 13 cloverleafs. Use the other 2 between the outer bead units.

Make 13 bead units.
Make 15 cloverleafs.
Attach each bead unit to a cloverleaf.

Make 2 wrap bead units with a Silver bead, a stone then a Silver bead.
Make 2 wrap bead units with a Silver bead, a 6mm bead then a Silver bead.

Cloverleaf and Blue Beads Necklace -

MATERIALS: 20 gauge Silver wire • 16 Blue 4mm beads • 20 Silver 2mm beads • 1 Blue 10mm x 16mm teardrop stone with a top hole • 1 Silver 14mm x 20mm teardrop metal disk • E6000 glue • jump rings

INSTRUCTIONS: Make 14 bead units (see page 3). Turn a loop in one end of the wire. Slide a Blue bead and Silver bead up the wire. Turn a loop in the other end of the wire. (Each bead unit uses about 1¹/2" of wire)..

Make 2 loop bead units. Turn a loop in one end of the wire. Slide a Silver, a Blue bead and a Silver bead up the wire. Turn a loop in the other end of the wire.

Make a spiral (see page 5). Hammer the spiral if desired. Thread the wire end through the hole in the top of the teardrop. Turn a loop in the end of the wire and wrap the wire end under the loop. (Each spiral uses about 3" of wire). Glue the stone to the metal disk.

Make 16 cloverleafs. Attach a stone unit to 14 cloverleafs. Use the other 2 between the outer bead units. (Each cloverleaf uses about 2" of wire).

Attach cloverleafs together with jump rings.

Make 14 bead units.
Make 16 cloverleafs.
Attach each bead unit to a cloverleaf.

Make 2 bead units with a Silver bead, a 4mm bead then a Silver bead.

Thread a spiral on the teardrop. Loop and wrap the wire end.

Cloverleaf, Spiral and Black Beads Necklace -

MATERIALS: 20 gauge Silver wire • 17 Black 4mm pearl beads • jump rings

INSTRUCTIONS: Make 17 bead units (see page 3). Turn a loop in one end of the wire. Slide a Black bead up the wire. Turn a loop in the other end of the wire. (Each bead unit uses about 1¹/2" of wire).

Make 15 spirals (see page 5). Hammer the spiral. if desired. Turn a loop in the end of the wire and twist the loop. (Each spiral uses about 3" of wire).

Attach a spiral to 13 bead units.

Make 19 cloverleafs. (Each cloverleaf uses about 2" of wire).

Attach a bead unit to 14 cloverleafs. Attach a spiral to 2 cloverleafs. Use the other 4 between the outer bead units.

Make 17 loop bead units.

Attach a cloverleaf and a spiral to a bead unit. Make 13.

Attach a spiral to a cloverleaf. Make 2.

Illustrations are shown actual size.

Easy Swirls for Beginners

What happens when you're working in one direction and change your mind to work in the other direction - you make a swirl, or a swirl in a frame or even a fancy spiral every now and then! When you do it on purpose, you end up with some really gorgeous jewelry!

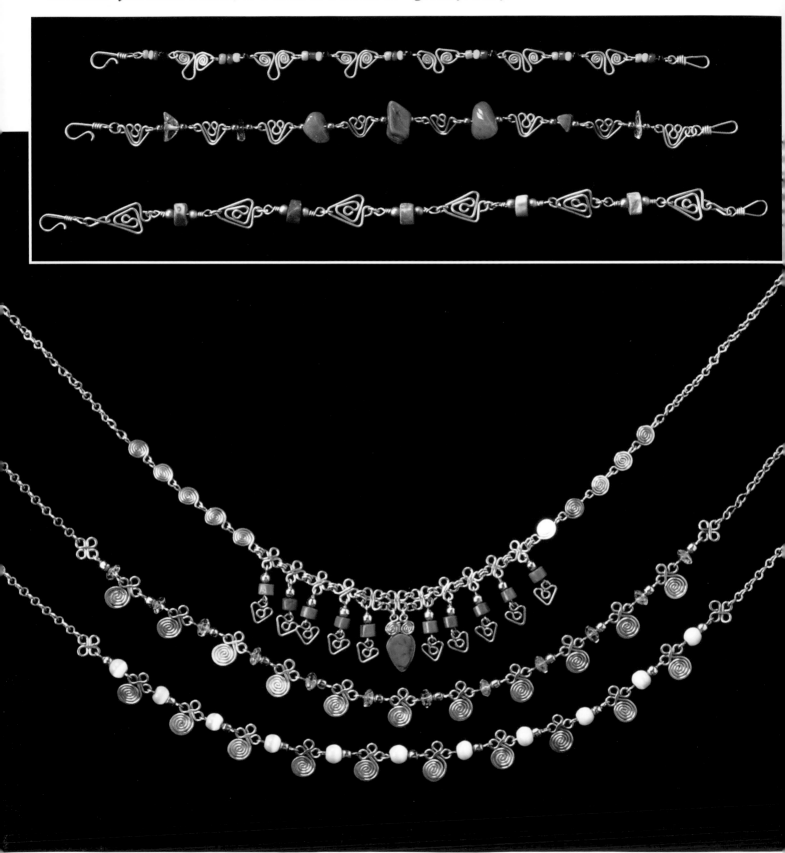

Swirls & Seed Beads Bracelet -

MATERIALS: 20 gauge Silver wire • Seed beads (7 Black, 7 Green, 7 Red, 7 Yellow) • jump rings

INSTRUCTIONS: Make 6 squiggle units. Turn a spiral at each end of the wire. Make a 2-sided triangle around the spiral. Bend the wire in the middle and bring the ends of the wire together at the top center. (Each squiggle unit uses about 2¹/₂" of wires.)

Make 7 loop bead units with the seed beads. Attach units with jump rings.

Turn a spiral at each end. Wrap 2 straight sides. Bend the center, fold up the ends. Make 7 bead units.

Curlicues & Stones Bracelet -

MATERIALS: 20 gauge Silver wire • 3 medium and 4 small Turquoise stones • 14 Black seed beads • jump rings

INSTRUCTIONS: Make 8 curlicue units. Turn a a loop in one end of the wire. Make another loop to one side and above it, then bend the wire back toward the top. Fold the wire down beside the first loop and back toward the top. Bend the wire back over the top and turn a loop in the end. (Each curclicue uses about 2" of wire).

Make a loop bead unit with each of the stones and 2 seed beads.
Attach units with jump rings.

Turn 3 loops at one end. Go over the top. Go back over the top and turn a loop in the end. Make 7 bead units.

Triangles & Stones Bracelet -

MATERIALS: 20 gauge Silver wire • 5 Toast-color 6mm beads • 10 Silver 2mm beads • jump rings

INSTRUCTIONS: Make 6 triangle units. Turn a loop in one end of the wire. Make another loop to one side and below it, then bend the wire back toward the top. Fold the wire down beside the first loop and back across the bottom. Bend the wire back over the top and down to the bottom. Turn a loop in the end. (Each triangle uses about 3" of wire).

Make a wrapped bead unit with each of the stones and 2 Silver beads.
Attach units with jump rings.

Turn 2 loops at one end. Go over the top. Go across the bottom. Bend outer triangle. Turn a loop in the end at the bottom Make 5 wrap bead units.

Triangles, Cloverleaves, Spirals & Stones Necklace -

MATERIALS: 20 gauge Silver wire • 1 Turquoise 8mm x 12mm teardrop stone • 10 Turquoise 6mm beads • 10 Silver 3mm beads• jump rings

INSTRUCTIONS: Make 10 triangle units. Turn a loop in one end of the wire. Make another loop to one side and just above it. Bend a triangle and turn a loop at the top. (Each triangle uses about 2" of wire).

Make 10 spirals according to the instructions on page 5, except after turning the top loop, hammer the spiral, bend the wire across the back and turn another loop in the end. Twist the bottom loop. (Each spiral uses about 3" of wire).

Make 11 cloverleafs (see page 5). (Each cloverleaf uses about 2" of wire).

Make 10 loop bead units with the small Turquoise and Silver beads. Attach the units to 10 of the cloverleafs as shown in the illustration.

Refer to the instructions on page 17 to wrap the teardrop. Attach the teardrop to 2 loops of a cloverleaf with 2 jump rings..

Use jumprings to attach the other 2 straight cloverleafs at either side of the center one. Use double jumprings to attach the remaining tilted cloverleafs and the first spiral at each side.

Attach units with jump rings.

Turn a top loop, bend the wire across the back. Turn a loop and twist it.

Make 10 bead units. Attach 8 of them to tilted cloverleafs.

Turn 2 loops, bend the wire in a triangle. Turn a loop at the end.

Attach 2 of the bead units to straight cloverleafs.

Refer to the instructions on page 17 to wrap the teardrop stone. Attach the top loops to 2 loops of a straight cloverleaf.

Cloverleaf, Spirals & Crystals Necklace -

MATERIALS: 20 gauge Silver wire • 12 Clear 5mm x 3mm crystal beads • 12 Silver 3mm beads• jump rings

INSTRUCTIONS: Make 11 spirals (see page 5), except instead of turning a top loop, bend a 3-petal cloverleaf at the top of each spiral. Follow the cloverleaf instruction (see page 5). (Each spiral uses about 3" of wire). Hammer each spiral if desired.

Make 2 cloverleafs (see page 5). (Each cloverleaf uses about 2" of wire).
Make 12 loop bead units (see page 3) with the beads.
Alternate bead units and spirals.
Attach units with jump rings.

Bend a 3-petal cloverleaf at the top of each spiral. Make 11.

Make 2 cloverleafs for the ends.

Make 12 bead units to alternate with spirals.

Cloverleaf, Spirals & Crystals Necklace -

MATERIALS: 20 gauge Silver wire • 11 Light Green 6mm beads • 11 Silver 3mm bead • jump rings

INSTRUCTIONS: Make 10 spirals (see page 5), except instead of turning a top loop, bend a 3-petal cloverleaf at the top of each spiral. (Each spiral uses about 2" of wire). Follow the cloverleaf instruction (see page 5). Hammer each spiral if desired.

Make 2 cloverleafs (see page 5).(Each cloverleaf uses about 2" of wire).
Make 11 loop bead units(see page 3) with the beads.
Alternate bead units and spirals.

Bend a 3-petal cloverleaf at the top of each spiral. Make 11.

Make 2 cloverleaves for the ends.

Make 11 bead units to alternate with spirals.

Wild and Wacky Wiggles

When you first begin working with wire to make jewelry you were probably surprised that you could make a cloverleaf! After all, isn't jewelry supposed to be about jewels, beads or stones?

Once it was, but as you know by now, it's a wonderful mixture of imaginative twists and turns - a true adventure in shaping and bending any way your whimsy turns!

These projects are combinations of beads, stones and new and familiar wire shapes. Enjoy!

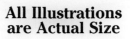

Loop-de-Loops, Wiggles & Stones Bracelet -

MATERIALS: 20 gauge Silver wire • 1 Clear 6mm x 15mm crystal bead • 1 decorative 15mm bead • 4 assorted small stones • 6 White 3mm pearl beads • jump rings
INSTRUCTIONS: Make 3 large bead units (see page 3). Turn a loop in one end of the wire. Slide a crystal stone, the seed beads and the 15mm crystal up the wire. Turn a loop at the other end. Cut away any excess wire. Repeat for the decorative bead, placing a small pearl at either end of the bead. (Each large bead unit uses about 2" of wire).

Make 3 small loop bead units (see page 3). Turn a a loop in one end of the wire. Slide a pearl and a stone up the wire. Turn a loop at the other end. Cut away excess wire. (Each small bead unit uses about 1" of wire).

Make 2 loop-de-loop units. Turn a 3-petal cloverleaf (see page 5). Bend the wire at an angle toward the bottom then bend it back and make a bottom loop as shown in the illustration. Bend the other side of the bottom portion in a mirror image of the first side. Cut away any excess wire. (Each loop-de-loop uses about 5" of wire).

Make 2 wiggles as shown. (Each wiggle uses about 4" of wire)

Make 1 cloverleaf (see page 5). (Each cloverleaf uses about 2" of wire).

Attach units together.

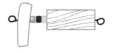 Make 2 large bead units. Use 2 pearls and a decorative bead of your choice for the other bead unit.

 Make 2 wiggles.

 Make 1 cloverleaf.

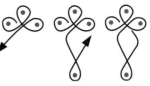 For loop-de-loops, make 3 leaves as for a cloverleaf. Bend the wire and make a lower loop, bend the wire back as shown. Make 2.

Squiggles & Seed Beads Bracelet -

MATERIALS: 20 gauge Silver wire • 7 Red seed beads • 14 Black seed beads • jump rings
INSTRUCTIONS: Make 7 bead units (see page 3). Turn a loop in one end of the wire. Slide a Black, a Red and a Black seed bead up the wire. Turn a loop at the other end. Cut away any excess wire. (Each loop bead unit uses about 1" of wire)

Make a small squiggles. Bend the wire back to the left above the coil as shown in the illustration. Bend the wire around the squiggle and back to the bottom. Turn a loop at the end. Cut away excess wire. (Each squiggle uses about 4" of wire).

Attach units together.

 For squiggles, make a small spiral. Bend the wire to make a loop, wrap the wire around the coil and back to the bottom. Turn a loop. Make 7.

 Make 7 bead units.

Spirals with a Cloverleaf Necklace -

MATERIALS: 20 gauge Silver wire • jump rings
INSTRUCTIONS: Make 29 spirals. (see page 5). Turn a loop at the top left above the spiral to make the first cloverleaf petal. Repeat to make 2 more petals. Cut away any excess wire. (Each spiral uses about 6" of wire).

Attach spirals with jump rings.

 Make a spiral and top it with 3 cloverleaf petals.

Spirals in a Box Necklace -

MATERIALS: 20 gauge Silver wire • jump rings
INSTRUCTIONS: Make 19 spirals (see page 5). Bend the wire down and across the bottom of the coil as shown in the illustration. Take the wire across the top and bend the wire back across the top. Turn a loop in the end of the wire. Cut away any excess wire. (Each spiral uses about 6" of wire).

Attach the spirals with jumprings.

 Make a spiral and bend a square around the spiral. Bend the wire back and turn a loop at the end.

Spirals in a Tilted Box Necklace -

MATERIALS: 20 gauge Silver wire • jump rings
INSTRUCTIONS: Make 17 spirals (see page 5). Bend the wire down at one side and bend the wire again at the bottom of the spiral as shown in the illustration. Take the wire up to the other side and bend it across the top. Bend the wire back across the top then bend it back to center it above the spiral. Turn a loop in the end of the wire. Cut away any excess wire. (Each spiral uses about 8" of wire).

Attach the spirals with jump rings.

 Make a spiral and bend a tilted square around it. Bend the wire across the top then bend it back again. Bend it back to the center and turn a loop at the end.

Wings, Cloverleafs & Beads Necklace -

MATERIALS: 20 gauge Silver wire • 14 Pink 6mm oat beads • jump rings
INSTRUCTIONS: Make 13 bead units (see page 3). Turn a loop in one end of the wire. Thread a bead onto the wire. Turn a loop at the other end. Cut away any excess wire. (Each bead unit uses about 1" of wire)..

Make 5 wings. Turn a loop at one end of the wire and make a larger loop below and just to the side of it. Bend the wire back down straight and turn another large and slightly longer loop. Make another larger and longer loop. Make 2 progressively shorter loops to make a mirror image of the first side. Turn a loop in the wire. Cut away any excess wire end. Fold the ends of each wing up in a semicircle to pinch the tops of the larger loops together.. (Each wing uses about 6" of wire)..

Make 4 cloverleafs. Use jumprings to attach a bead unit between 2 cloverleafs. Add 11 bead units with jumprings. Attach a cloverleaf, a bead unit and a cloverleaf. on each side. (Each cloverleaf uses about 2" of wire)..

Attach a wing to the center bead unit. Place 2 wings on each side leafing a bead unit between the wings.

MAKE A WIGGLE: Turn a loop at one end and make a loose loop below it. Bend the wire down and make a loose loop. Make an even longer loose loop. Make 2 loose loops in a mirror image of the first 2 loose loops. Turn a loop at the end. Bend the loops up and together in a semicircle to close the tops of the loose loops.

 Make 13 bead units.

 Make 4 cloverleaves.

Terrific Twisted Frames and Twirls

Making jewelry with wire is an experience much like learning how to drive! At first you're afraid to do anything different; then you can't wait to get out there on an open road!

Turquoise Beads in a Small Square Frame Necklace -

MATERIALS: 20 gauge Silver wire • 12 Turquoise 6mm beads • jump rings
INSTRUCTIONS: Slide beads on the end of wire. Begin at the top left corner and wrap the wire in a square shape around a bead. Make another square around the bead and loop the wire above and beyond the square at the top left corner
Turn a loop so the wire goes back over and extends past the top right corner of the square. Turn a loop in the end of the wire to attach it to the next frame. Twist the loop flat. (Each bead unit uses about 3" of wire).
Attach units with jump rings.

Fold a double square around the bead.

Make a loop at each side of the square top. Twist the loop flat.

Blue Beads in a Slanted Square Frame Necklace -

MATERIALS: 20 gauge Silver wire • 11 Blue 4mm beads • jump rings
INSTRUCTIONS: Make 12 squares. Slide a bead up the wire. Begin to wrap the wire in a square shape around the bead. Make another square around the bead. Turn a loop in the end of the wire to attach it to a spiral. Twist the loop flat. Hammer the spirals flat. if desired. (Each bead unit uses about 3" of wire).
Make 12 spirals, leaving the bottom loop open as shown. Turn a loop in the end of the wire. (Each spiral uses about 3" of wire)
Attach spirals to squares with jump rings.

Turn a loop, thread bead. Fold a double square around bead. Turn a loop, twist it flat.

Make 12 spirals with an open bottom loop.

Telephone Rectangles Bracelet -

MATERIALS: 20 gauge Silver wire • 5 Coral and 2 White 4mm beads • jump rings
INSTRUCTIONS: Make 8 telephone rectangles. Turn a loop in the end of the wire and wrap the wire in a rectangle shape around the loop. Make 2 more rectangles around the first one. Turn a loop so the wire goes back over to extend past the top. (Each rectangle uses about 5" of wire).
Make 7 bead units (see page 3) with one bead in the center of each. Turn a loop in the end of the wire to attach it to the next bead unit. Attach units together.

Make 8 telephone-shaped rectangles.

Make 5 Coral and 2 White bead units.

Green Beads in a Square Frame Necklace -

MATERIALS: 20 gauge Silver wire • 21 Green 5mm beads • jump rings
INSTRUCTIONS: Make 14 large squares. Turn a loop in the end of the wire and wrap the wire in a square shape around a loop with a bead. Make 2 more squares around the first one. Turn a loop so the wire goes back over to extend past the top. Turn a loop in the end of the wire to attach it to the next bead unit. (Each square uses about 6" of wire). Attach units together.

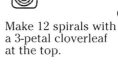

Make 21 squares.

Blue Beads and Spirals in a Frame Necklace -

MATERIALS: 20 gauge Silver wire • 9 Blue 5mm beads • jump rings
INSTRUCTIONS: Make 12 spirals with cloverleaf tops. Roll a spiral in the end of the wire. Hammer the spirals if desired.
Make 9 rectangle units. Slide a bead up the wire. Wrap the wire in a rectangle shape around the bead. Fold the wire back over to extend past the top. Turn a loop in the end of the wire to attach it to the next frame. (Each unit uses about 3 1/2" of wire). Attach units together.

Make 9 rectangles.

Make 12 spirals with a 3-petal cloverleaf at the top.

Blue Seed Beads in a Triangle Necklace -

MATERIALS: 20 gauge Silver wire • 30 Blue seed beads • jump rings
INSTRUCTIONS: Make 30 units following the illustrations. Bend over one end of the wire and slide a bead up the wire. Begin to wrap wire in a triangle shape around the bead. Make a total of 3 triangles around each bead, each with a point lower than the one before.. Make a loop in the wire at one side and extend the wire back across the top. Turn a loop in the end of the wire to attach it to the shape. Twist the loop flat. (Each unit uses about 2 1/2" of wire).
Attach units together.

Make 30 triangles with a seed bead, following the steps below..

 1. Bend end of the wire, thread bead.
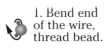 2. Bend a triangle around the bead.
 3. Bend another triangle around the bead.
 4. Bend another triangle.
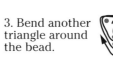 5. Bend a loop at the corner, go back across top.

Blue Beads in a Triangle Necklace -

MATERIALS: 18 gauge Silver wire • 11 Blue 3mm beads • jump rings
INSTRUCTIONS: Make 22 triangle units following the illustrations above. Bend over one end of the wire and thread a bead on the wire. Make a total of 3 triangles around each bead, each with a point lower than the one before. Make a loop in the wire at one side and extend the wire back across the top. Turn a loop in the end of the wire to attach it to a spiral. Twist the loop flat. (Each unit uses about 3 1/2" of wire). Attach units together.

6. Turn a loop at the other corner. Twist loop flat.

Fancy Triangles Necklace -

MATERIALS: 20 gauge Silver wire • 1 Turquoise 18mm teardrop stone or disk • jump rings
INSTRUCTIONS: Make 10 triangle units. Turn a loop in the end of the wire then twist 2 more loops. Begin to wrap the wire in a triangle. Make 2 more triangles. Turn a flat loop in the end of the wire to attach it to the next triangle. Twist the loop flat. (Each unit uses about 3" of wire).
CENTER STONE: Cut 4" of wire. See Necklace 5 on page 17 to wrap the stone.

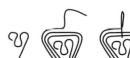
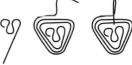

Make triangles around center curlicue.

Super Sunbursts and Suns

You're not supposed to hide your light under a bushel, so here's a chance to shine, shine, shine!

Create dozens of shining sunbursts and sun jewelry pieces with wire!

Sunbursts & Blue Beads Bracelet -
MATERIALS: 20 gauge Silver wire • 3 Blue 5mm beads • 10 Toast 4mm bugle beads • 20 Silver 3mm beads • jump rings

INSTRUCTIONS: Make 10 bead units (see page 3). Turn a loop in one end of the wire. Slide a Silver, a bugle and another Silver bead up the wire. Turn a loop at the other end. Cut away any excess wire. (Each loop bead unit uses about 2" of wire).

 Make 10 bead units.

 Thread a bead on the wire bend a crimp in the wire. Turn a loop.

Make 3 sunburst units. Slide a Blue bead to one end of the wire and leave about ¹/₂" of wire sticking out from the bead. Bend the wire down on the other side of the bead and turn a loop just above the bend. This crimp will keep the bead securely in place while you complete the sunburst. Continue turning loops around the bead until you make 6 turned loops. Before turning the next loop, use the other end of the wire to turn a loop over the working wire on the other side of the sunburst. Continue to turn a total of 11 loops. Before turning the last loop, hook the working wire over the beginning crimp. Cut away excess wire. (Each sunburst unit uses about 6" of wire).

 Turn 5 more loops. Loop the other end of the wire over the working wire in the 7th loop.

Attach 4 bead units together at one end, then alternate bead units with the sunbursts in the center. Finish with 4 more bead units.

Turn a total of 11 loops. Loop the end of the working wire over the crimp, turn the last loop.

Spiral Sunbursts & Black Beads Bracelet -
MATERIALS: 20 gauge Silver wire • 8 Black 5mm barrel beads • jump rings

INSTRUCTIONS: Make 8 bead units. Turn a loop in one end of the wire. Slide a bead up the wire. Turn a loop at the other end. Cut away any excess wire. (Each loop bead unit uses about 2" of wire)

Make 5 spiral sunbursts. Make a ¹/₄" spiral (see page 5). Hammer the spiral if desired. Turn a loop in the wire and continue around the outside edge of the spiral to turn 10 loops. Cut away excess wire. Wrap and crimp a piece of wire around the first and last loop to secure. (Each spiral sunburst unit uses about 9" of wire)

Attach a bead unit to 2 chain links, then alternate bead units with the sunbursts in the center. Finish with a bead unit, 3 chain links and another bead unit.

 Make 8 bead units.

Make 5 spiral sunbursts with 10 loops. Secure the first and last loops with a piece of wire.

Spiral Sunbursts & Turquoise Beads Necklace -
MATERIALS: 18 gauge Silver wire • 16 Turquoise 5mm pearl beads • 32 Silver 3mm beads • jump rings

INSTRUCTIONS: Make 16 bead units (see page 3). Turn a loop in one end of the wire. Thread a Silver, Turquoise and another Silver bead onto the wire. Turn a loop at the other end. Cut away any excess wire. (Each loop bead unit uses 1 to 2" of wire)

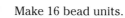 Make 16 bead units.

Make 1 large sunburst spiral with the loops around the outer edge. For the center make a ³/₈" spiral (see page 5). Hammer the spiral if desired. Turn a loop in the wire and continue around the outside edge of the spiral to turn 8 loops. Bend the end of the wire around the first loop to secure the first and last loop. Cut away excess wire. (The large sunburst spiral unit uses about 10" of wire)

 Make 1 sunburst with 8 loops around the outside of the spiral. Hook the wire end over first loop.

Make 10 smaller spiral sunbursts with the loops overlapping the outer edge.. Make a ¹/₂" spiral (see page 5). Hammer spiral if desired. Turn a loop in the wire and bend it down to overlap the outer edge of the spiral. Continue around to turn 8 loops. Bend the end of the wire around the first loop to secure. Cut away excess wire. (Each smaller sunburst spiral unit uses about 9" of wire)

 Make 10 sunbursts with 8 loops that overlap the outer edges of the spiral. Hook the end of the wire over the first loop.

At each end, alternate 4 bead units with 3 overlapping sunbursts. Attach 2 bead units to the last overlapping sunburst, add another overlapping sunburst and then 2 bead units. Use the larger sunburst in the center. Finish the other end in a mirror image of the first side.

Spiral Sunbursts & Red Beads Necklace -
MATERIALS: 20 gauge Silver wire • 11 Red 5mm beads • 19 Silver 3mm beads • jump rings

INSTRUCTIONS: Make 8 bead units with 1 Red and 2 Silver beads. Make 3 bead units with only 1 Red and 1 Silver bead. Turn a loop in one end of the wire. Slide a Silver, a Red and another Silver bead up the wire. Turn a loop at the other end. Cut away excess wire. (Each loop bead unit uses 1 to 2" of wire)

Make 3 bead units with only 1 Red and 1 Silver bead. Turn a loop in one end of the wire. Slide a Silver and a Red bead up the wire. Turn a loop at the other end. Cut away excess wire. (Each unit uses 1 to 2" of wire)

For the center spiral sunburst, cut a 10" piece of wire. Make a ³/₈" spiral (see page 5). Hammer the spiral if desired. Turn a loop in the wire and continue around the outside edge of the spiral to turn 10 loops. Cut away excess wire. Wrap and crimp a piece of wire around the first and last loops to secure.

Alternate sunbursts with 3-bead units. Attach the 2-bead units to the center 3 sunbursts.

Make 8 units with 3 beads.

Make 3 bead units with 2 beads for center suns.

 Make 9 spiral sunbursts with 10 loops. Secure first and last loops with a piece of wire.

Suns & Blue Beads Bracelet -
MATERIALS: 20 gauge Silver wire • 9 Bright Blue 6mm beads • jump rings

INSTRUCTIONS: Make 10 rays for each sun (90 total). Turn a ¹/₈" loop in one end of the wire. Turn a narrow ¹/₄" tall loop, then turn another ¹/₈" loop on the other side of the tall loop. Cut away excess wire. (Each ray uses about 2" of wire)

Thread 10 rays onto a 3" piece of wire and pull the rays into a circle. Twist one wire tail around the wire where they meet. Fold the longer wire end across the center of the sun, slide a bead onto the wire and bend the wire end over the threading wire. Make 9 suns.

Attach the suns together with jump rings.

Turn a ¹/₈" loop, a ¹/₄" tall loop and a ¹/₈" loop. Make 9 rays for each sun.

Thread 10 rays onto wire, bend into a circle. Secure one end, thread a bead, bend end over the other side.

Suns, Cones and Turquoise Beads Necklace -
MATERIALS: 20 gauge Silver wire • 7 Turquoise 4mm cat's eye beads • jump rings

INSTRUCTIONS: Make 14 rays for each sun (98 total). Make each ray with a ¹/₈" loop and a ³/₈" tall loop. Turn a ¹/₈" loop at one end. Turn a narrow ³/₈" tall loop, then turn another ¹/₈" loop. Cut away excess wire. (Each ray uses about 2" of wire)

Make 7 cones. Coil wire around a pencil tip to make each cone. (Each uses about 3" of wire)

Make 7 suns. Thread 14 rays onto a 4" wire and pull wire into a circle. Twist the ends together. Insert one end in a cone, turn a loop at the top. Fold the other end across the center of the sun, slide bead in place then bend the end of wire over the other side.

Attach the suns together with jump rings.

 Turn a ¹/₈", ³/₈" and a ¹/₈" loop for the first ray. Make 14 rays with two ¹/₈" and one ³/₈" loop.

 Coil wire around a pencil tip to make 7 cones.

 Thread rays, bend into a circle. Twist ends, thread a bead on one end, bend over the other side. Loop other end above a cone.

Easy Scrolls for Beginners

Imagine white sandy beaches, cool evening breezes, lilting tropical music and some exotic beverage with a little umbrella in it.

That's the feeling you'll have when you wear these romantic combinations of beads, stones and shiny Silver wire.

Spirals, Wiggles, Leaves and Bead Necklace -

MATERIALS: 20 gauge Silver wire • 1 Turquoise 10mm x 15mm oval stone • E6000 glue • jump rings
INSTRUCTIONS: Attach together with jump rings.

Make 4 spirals (see page 5), except instead of turning a top loop, bend a 3-petal cloverleaf at one side of each spiral (see page 5). Bend wire in a crook at the back of spiral. Make a cloverleaf at the other side of the spiral. Bend the wire in a crook at the back of the spiral. Cut away excess wire. Do not hammer spirals. (Each spiral uses about 4" of wire).

Refer to instructions on page 5 to make a 9-circle leaf. Make 2.

≡

Refer to instructions on page 3 to make a coil. Make 1 with 4 circles.

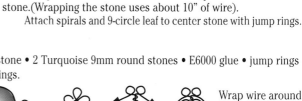

WRAP THE STONE: See page 11 for instructions to make a wiggle about 2" long in the middle of the wire to fit around the stone. Wrap the wiggle around the stone and glue in place. Thread the ends through the coil and turn a spiral in each end. Fold the spirals down to the stone.(Wrapping the stone uses about 10" of wire).

Attach spirals and 9-circle leaf to center stone with jump rings.

Spirals, Wiggles, Leaves and Bead Necklace -

MATERIALS: 20 gauge Silver wire • 1 Turquoise 8mm x 12mm teardrop stone • 2 Turquoise 9mm round stones • E6000 glue • jump rings
INSTRUCTIONS: Make all wire shapes then attach together with jump rings.

Make 16 spirals (see page 5), except instead of turning a top loop, bend a square petal at one side on the top of each spiral. Bend 3 more square petals across the top. Cut away excess wire. Hammer pieces. (Each spiral uses about 7" of wire).

Turn a loop in the center and twist the wire once. Wrap ends around stone and turn a loop in one end. wrap ends around wires. (Each round stone uses about 8" of wire). Make 2.

Make 1 cloverleaf (page 5) with about 2" of wire.

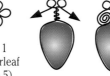

Wrap wire around the stone and glue. Twist wire at the top. Turn a loop in each wire end and make a spiral in each end next to stone. (Each stone uses about 7" of wire). Make 1.

Spirals, Cloverleaves and Beads Necklace -

MATERIALS: 20 gauge Silver wire • 1 Turquoise 20mm x 22mm teardrop stone • 12 Turquoise 4mm barrel beads • 12 Silver 3mm beads • E6000 glue • jump rings
INSTRUCTIONS: Make all wire shapes then attach together with jump rings.

Make a spiral (see page 5). Hammer the spiral if desired. Turn a loop at the top of the spiral and bend the wire down across the back to the bottom. Turn a loop in the end of the wire and twist the loop. (Each spiral uses about 5" of wire).Make 8 spirals.

Make cloverleaf.s (see page 5) with about 2" of wire. Make 13.

Make bead units (page 3) with about 1" of wire. Make 12.

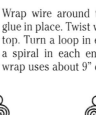

Wrap wire around the teardrop stone and glue in place. Twist wire ends together at the top. Turn a loop in each wire end and make a spiral in each end next to stone. (Each wrap uses about 9" of wire).

Spirals, Cloverleaves, Leaves and Stones Necklace -

MATERIALS: 20 gauge Silver wire • 1 Blue 13mm round stone • 2 Turquoise 7mm x 10mm teardrop stones • Flat Silver dangle • E6000 glue • jump rings
INSTRUCTIONS: Make all wire shapes then attach together with jump rings.

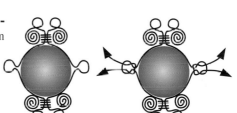

Cut 2 pieces of wire about 7" long for each teardrop. Center the stone on the wires and thread wire ends through a 4- circle coil at each side. Make a spiral (see page 5) in each wire end and fold spirals down to touch the stone. Cut away excess wire.

Refer to the instructions at the top of the page to make 2 double clover-leaf spirals.

See page 5 to make a 9-circle leaf. Make 1.

Cut 2 pieces of wire about 9" long for the round stone. Wrap stone and make spirals as for the teardrops, except leave a loop at each side of the stone. Cut 2 pieces of wire 5" long. Fold each in half and pull the ends through the side loops. Make a spiral in each end.

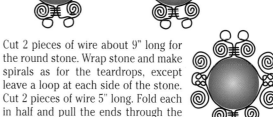

Spirals, Wings and Stones Necklace -

MATERIALS: 20 gauge Silver wire • 1 Turquoise 16mm round stone • 4 Turquoise nuggets • 4 Silver 3mm beads • Optional: E6000 glue • jump rings
INSTRUCTIONS: Make all wire shapes then attach together with jump rings.

Make 2 cloverleafs, each with about 2" of wire.

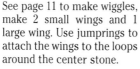

Cut 2" of wire to make 2 bead units. Wrap ends around wire below loops.

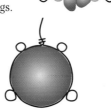

Refer to the instructions above to make 8 double-loop spirals.

See page 11 to make wiggles, make 2 small wings and 1 large wing. Use jumprings to attach the wings to the loops around the center stone.

Cut an 8" piece of wire to wrap the center stone. Make 2 loops 3/8" on either side of the center of the wire.

Make 2 loops 3/4" above the first 2. Insert stone and glue. Wrap wire at top.

Make a spiral with one end. Cut off the other end.

Fold spiral down on the stone, forming a loop.

Suns & Blue Beads Earrings -

MATERIALS: 20 gauge Silver wire • 2 Bright Blue 6mm beads • 2 ear wires • jump rings

INSTRUCTIONS:
See page 15 to make a sun for each earring. See page 9 to make a spiral with a cloverleaf top. Attach with jump rings.

Wiggles & Beads Earrings -

MATERIALS: 20 gauge Silver wire • 2 Tan 6mm beads • 2 ear wires • jump rings

INSTRUCTIONS:
See page 11 to make a wiggle for each earring.

Make a bead unit with about 3" of wire. Make a short wiggle then slide the bead up the wire. Turn a loop in the wire end. Cut away excess wire. Make 1 bead unit. for each earring.

Dangling Turquoise Beads Earrings -

MATERIALS: 20 gauge Silver wire • 6 Turquoise 6mm beads • 6 Silver 3mm beads • 2 ear wires • jump rings

INSTRUCTIONS:
See page 7 to make a dangle bead unit for each earring.

For the wire dangle, cut 6" of wire. Bend the wire in the center and overlap the ends to make a large bottom loop. Turn 2 loops on each side, overlap the wire ends again. Twist the wire ends, turn a loop in one and wrap the other end around the twists below the loop.

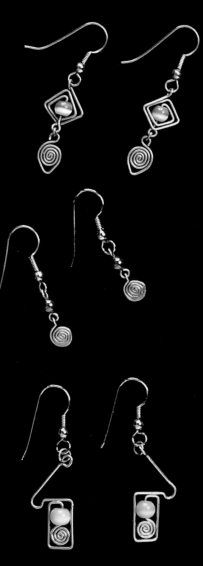

Spiral Sunburst & Black Bead Earrings -

MATERIALS: 20 gauge Silver wire • 2 Black 4mm beads • 2 ear wires • jump rings

INSTRUCTIONS: See page 15 make a 10-loop spiral sunburst f each earring. Make a bead unit wi 1" of wire for each earring.

Triangles & Beads Earrings -

MATERIALS: 20 gauge Silver wire • Turquoise 6mm beads • 2 Silv 3mm beads • 2 ear wires • jump rin

INSTRUCTIONS: See page 9 make a triangle and bead unit p earring.

Blue Beads in a Slanted Square Frame Earrings -

MATERIALS: 20 gauge Silver wi • 2 Blue 4mm beads • 2 ear wires jump rings

INSTRUCTIONS: See page 13 make a framed bead and ope looped spiral. for each earring.

Cloverleaf, Spiral & Black Bead Earrings

MATERIALS: 20 gauge Silver wi • 2 Black 4mm pearls • 2 ear wires jump rings

INSTRUCTIONS: See pages 3 - to make a cloverleaf, bead unit a spiral.

Blue Bead & Spirals in Frame Earrings -

MATERIALS: 20 gauge Silver wi • 2 Blue 5mm beads • 2 ear wires jump rings

INSTRUCTIONS: See page 13 make a framed bead and spiral. not bend the wire back over t top, but bend it at an angle. Turn loop in the end and twist the loop